You Caught Me KISSING

You Caught Me KISSING

a love story by
Dorothy Bridges

iBooks
Habent Sua Fata Libelli

A Publication iBooks

Copyright © 2005 Dorothy Bridges

iBooks
1230 Park Avenue, 8a
New York, NY 10128
bricktower@aol.com
www.BrickTowerPress.com

ISBN: 978-1-59687-311-7
First trade paper printing,
November 2011

Jacket and book desighn:
Jana Anderson, studio A design
www.studioadesign.biz

Dedicated
to my one and only

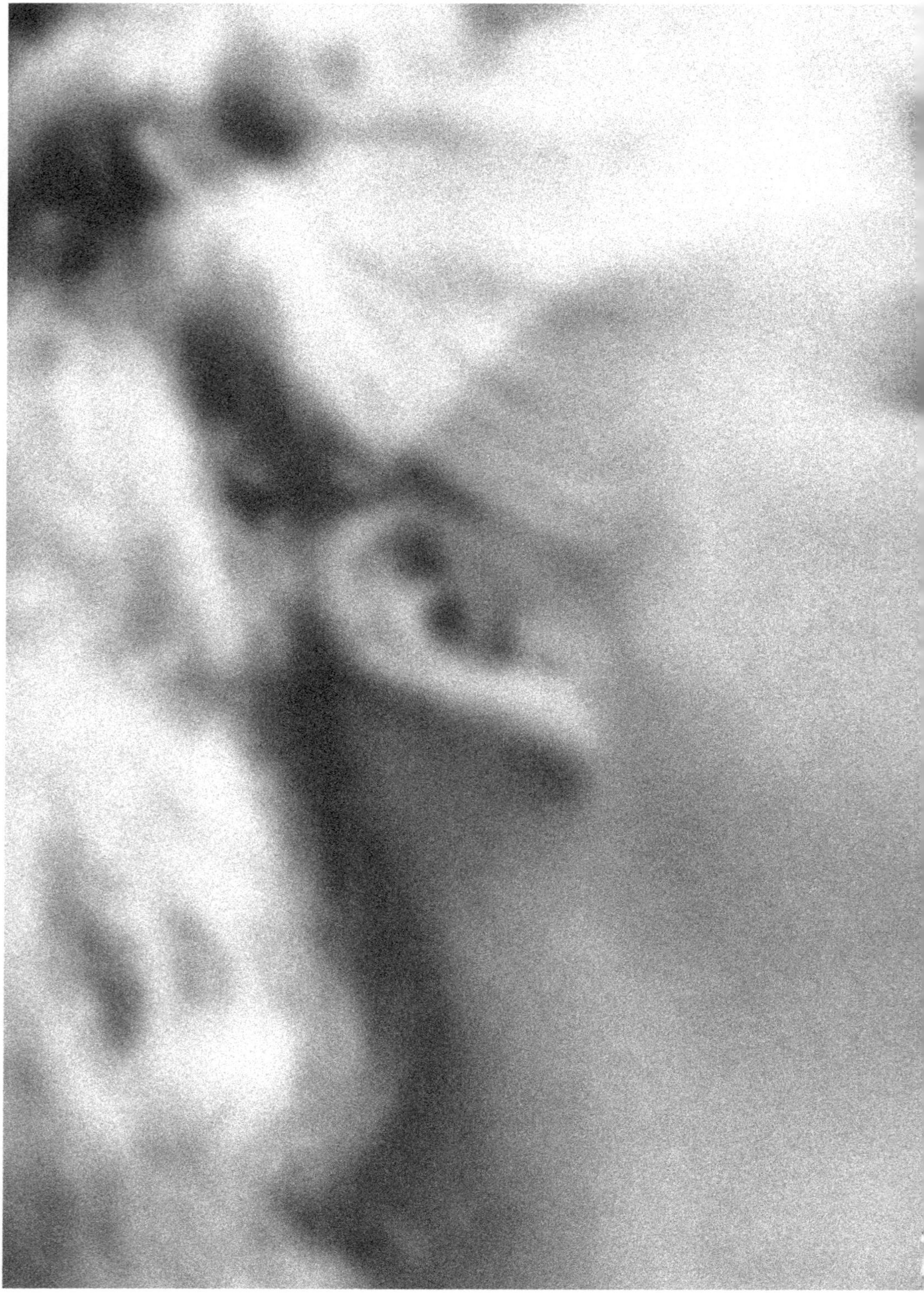

Beau Bridges

My mom has always been the family game organizer and all around cheerleader. Many of her favorite activities have to do with words: Scrabble, charades, crossword puzzles, and so on.

One of her favorite games with us kids began with the following phrase, "It was a dark and stormy night, when a band of robbers were sitting around a campfire talking. One of the robbers said, 'Leader, tell us a story,' and so he began." The next person would then repeat the sentence but with the first consonant in the alphabet (B) before each word. The new phrasing would be, "Bit Buzz Ba Bark Band Bormy Bight," and so forth. This would continue until we had gone through all the consonants in the alphabet. "Z" was one of my favorites as a child. "F" was a favorite as a teenager for reasons that will become obvious when tried.

My mom also read to us constantly when we were younger. As a twelve-year-old, I'll never forget listening to Barrie's "Peter Pan." A trip to London followed (my dad was making a movie there). While Dad worked, Mom and I visited Peter Pan's statue, Shakespeare's home, and countless other legendary sights in the world of English literature. I have such wonderful recollections from those formative years that definitely influenced my appreciation for words and stories today.

She has written poems for all of her children. I can still speak from memory most of the ones she wrote for me. One of them was: "I saw a squirrel with a woofy tail go whistling up a tree. He cracked a nut with his two front teeth and dropped the shells on me!"

Whether playing games together, reading stories, or writing poetry, my mom instilled in us all a tremendous sense of the importance of family as well as the value of expressions of love. How lucky I am to have this devoted, loving, vital, humorous, gifted lady as my mother!

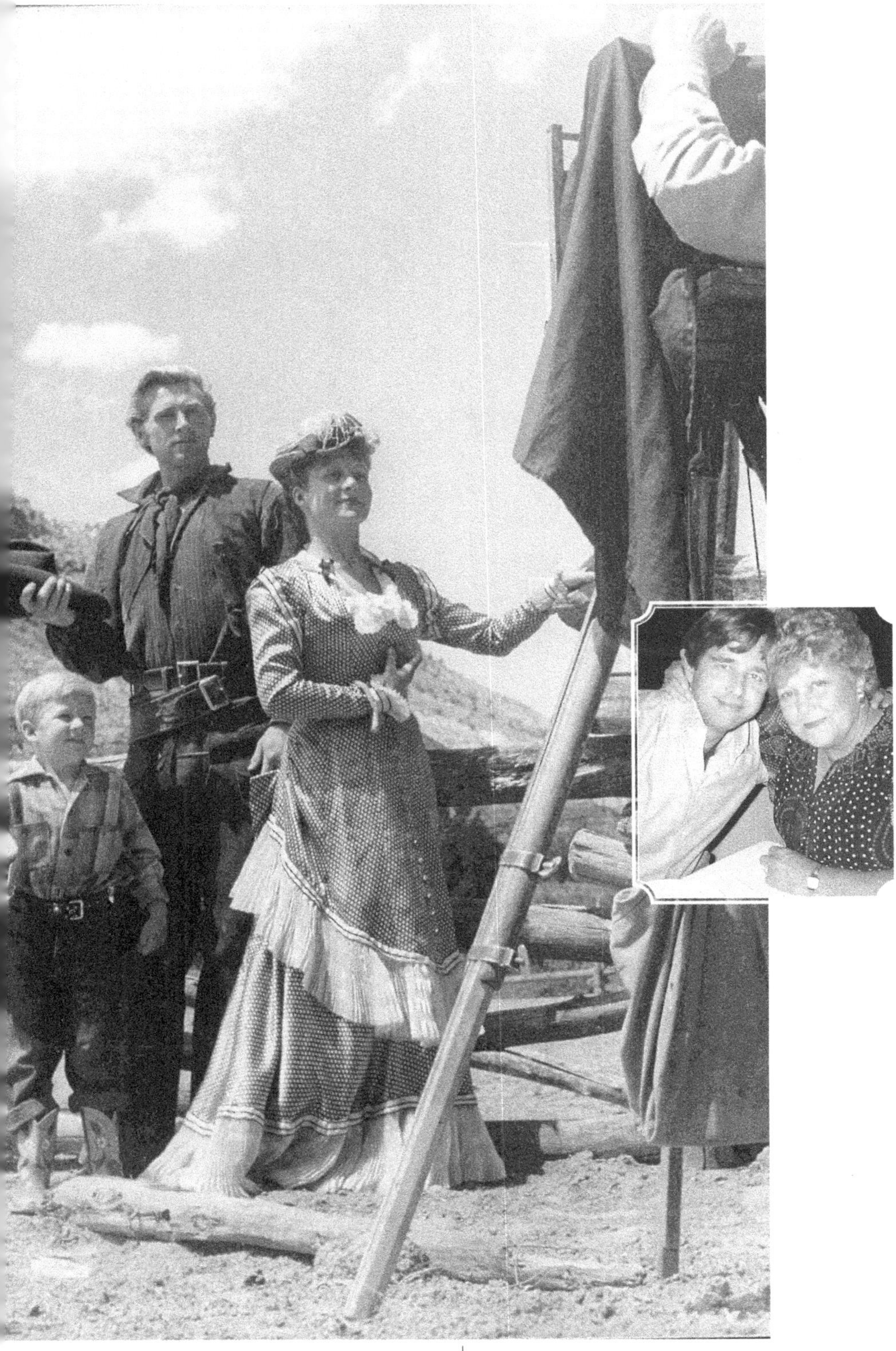

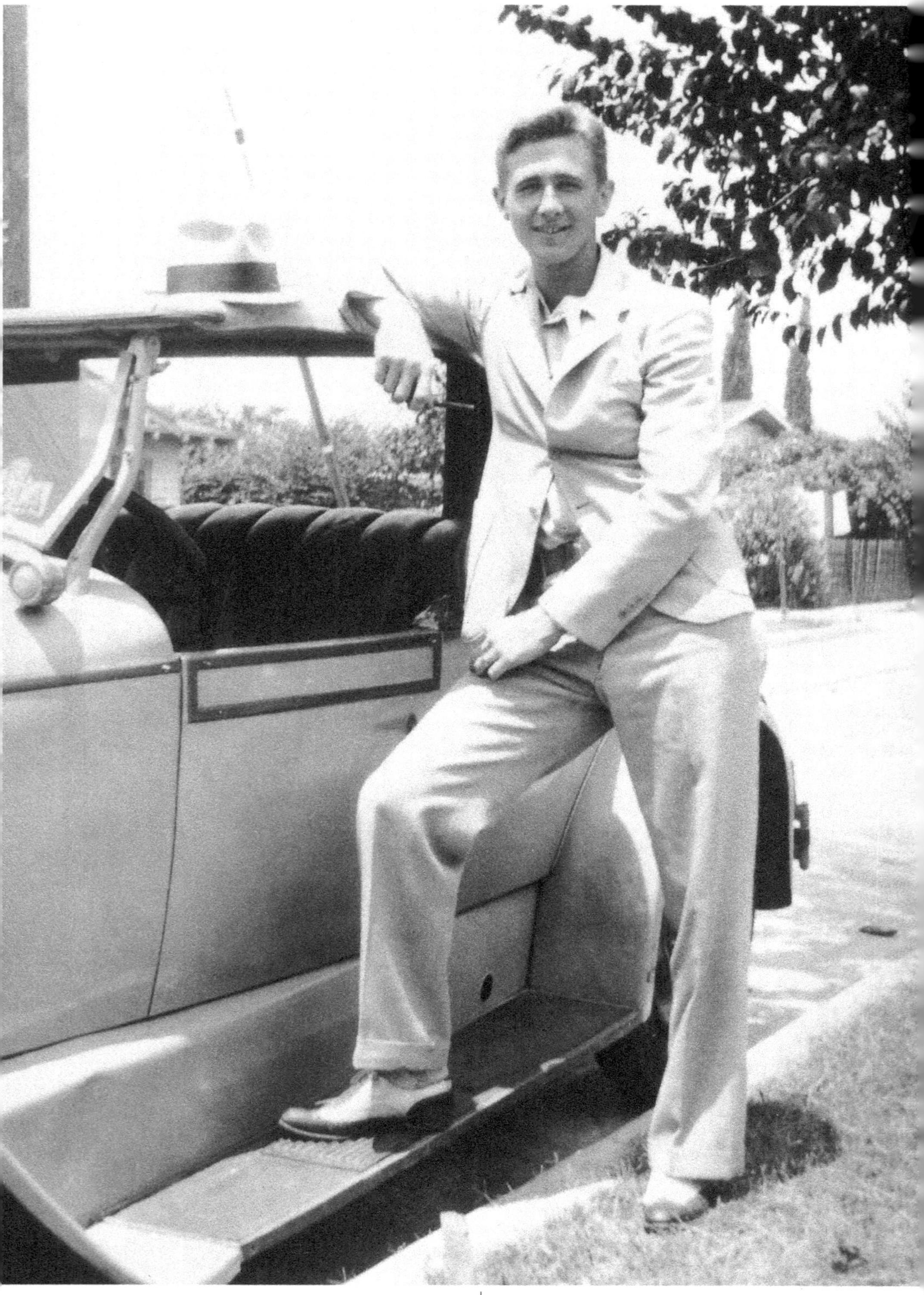

A while ago I went over to Mom's house—the one our family moved to after Dad scored big with *Sea Hunt*—a TV show he made in the early Sixties. She handed me something she had recently found—a book. She said, "Look at this." It was an old copy of *The Prophet*, by Gibran. I read it in high school and told her it was a favorite of mine. "Look inside," she said. I opened it and there on the first page was an inscription: 'To my sweetheart on her eighteenth birthday— Love, Lloyd.' The book was given to my mom as a gift from my dad. 'My God,' I thought, 'they have been loving each other a long time.' He gave it to her on September 19, 1933, only a couple of blocks from where we were sitting. The house we grew up in is just a short walk from where Mom and Dad met and courted each other—U.C.L.A. Dad was the head of the University Dramatic Society, and Mom was a freshman. She was encouraged to dance with him at a sorority party. My brother, sister and I have heard many stories about those days. One of my favorites is about the night of their first date. It was a double date. My dad's friend and his date were riding in front while my mom and dad made out in the rumble seat. I love that—the rumble seat—I wish they still had those. As my dad walked her to the door he said, "You don't know how to kiss." "What do you mean?!," she asked. "When you kiss," Dad said, "you 'say' prunes and you should 'say' apricots."

I guess they figured out the kissing part and a whole bunch of other things in the 62 years they were married. Some other things they didn't figure out, but that didn't stop them from loving each other. Like other couples that last that long they had their ups and downs, but were able to bend and stretch and not break. That's what I love about marriage—it's The Great Context. So much can go on inside it and, as the man says, 'what doesn't kill you makes you stronger.'

These Valentines can be read as a journal of a life long romance. I think of my mother as something of a master journalist. She's kept a diary every day of her life since her wedding day. When my brother, sister and I each turned twenty-one, we received a remarkable gift from our mom. She gave each of us a handwritten biography of our own lives; excerpts from her diaries. In other words, every time we were mentioned, she would transcribe the entry into our personal volume. What a gift, to have your life story told from your mother's point of view, written in her own hand. She's truly a remarkable woman and I'm so pleased to be able to share her with you.

Lucinda Bridges

I f I would draw my mother, the line would be in charcoal—the enduring bold mark of her strength and ability to blend, underscored by the initial ember of her warmth and random tongue of wit and fire. At eighty-nine she continues to inspire and amaze us all.

Dorothy Louise Simpson Bridges nurtured our family that became a garden. She tended us as unique souls and set us free in a landscape of unconditional love. She was the epitome of a Fifties homemaker; she cooked, she cleaned, and stayed at home raising three children while Daddy went off to work. He came home to homecooked meals, his kids jumping eagerly all over him to play, and he did, never too tired to wrestle, dance, or sing. I loved to prepare with Mom in the kitchen and watch her hold court with many a cocktail party— smoked oysters with colored toothpicks, pigs in a blanket and those little meatballs, martinis or mimosas. It wasn't unusual to end up having impromptu games or performances with friends who would come by. A special memory was watching from my spot under the coffee table listening to Meredith Wilson share some new tunes he had been working on for *The Music Man*. Mom would orchestrate the evenings, encouraging those who were unfamiliar or timid with 'on-the-spot' fun. Her fascination with what you had to share, your story, your joke, your song, was what I remember most. Midst it all, she would clean up, have us in bed (often with a song or story) and off to school the next morning with a favorite sack lunch. This was Her performance art. She was the hub of our family wheel. We called her 'the General,' not the corporal sort just in charge, more with a wand or a baton.

Ever so slowly she has been passing the baton down to us children. . .but she still wears those stripes and medals!! When challenge has come, she met it. I watched and learned how to remain centered in Love (in the hub) and let the spinning world do its impermanent twirl. My father always wanted her to publish her works. I think she felt she wasn't 'really' a writer, but continued to write poetry and prose privately through the years. The mother, the wife, the lover, the cook, the nurse, the teacher—they roll up together and take on a new role. Now must be the time for the writer.

These specific poems are a glimpse into the journey of a couple that stayed onboard their 'partner' ship. Through all kinds of weather they came back to the garden they created from the beginning.

You Caught Me Kissing, so I might as well let you see what happens to a girl who admits that every aspect of love has directed her life and destiny, from Puppy Love to the Grand Passion, to the Family Fortress, to Man Overboard, and continuing with There Has To Be Forever. ❧ My tale is easy to tell because there just happened to be one man involved, Lloyd Bridges, and all my life I kept writing love poems. ❧ Perhaps some of them tell your own love story.

Dorothy Bridges

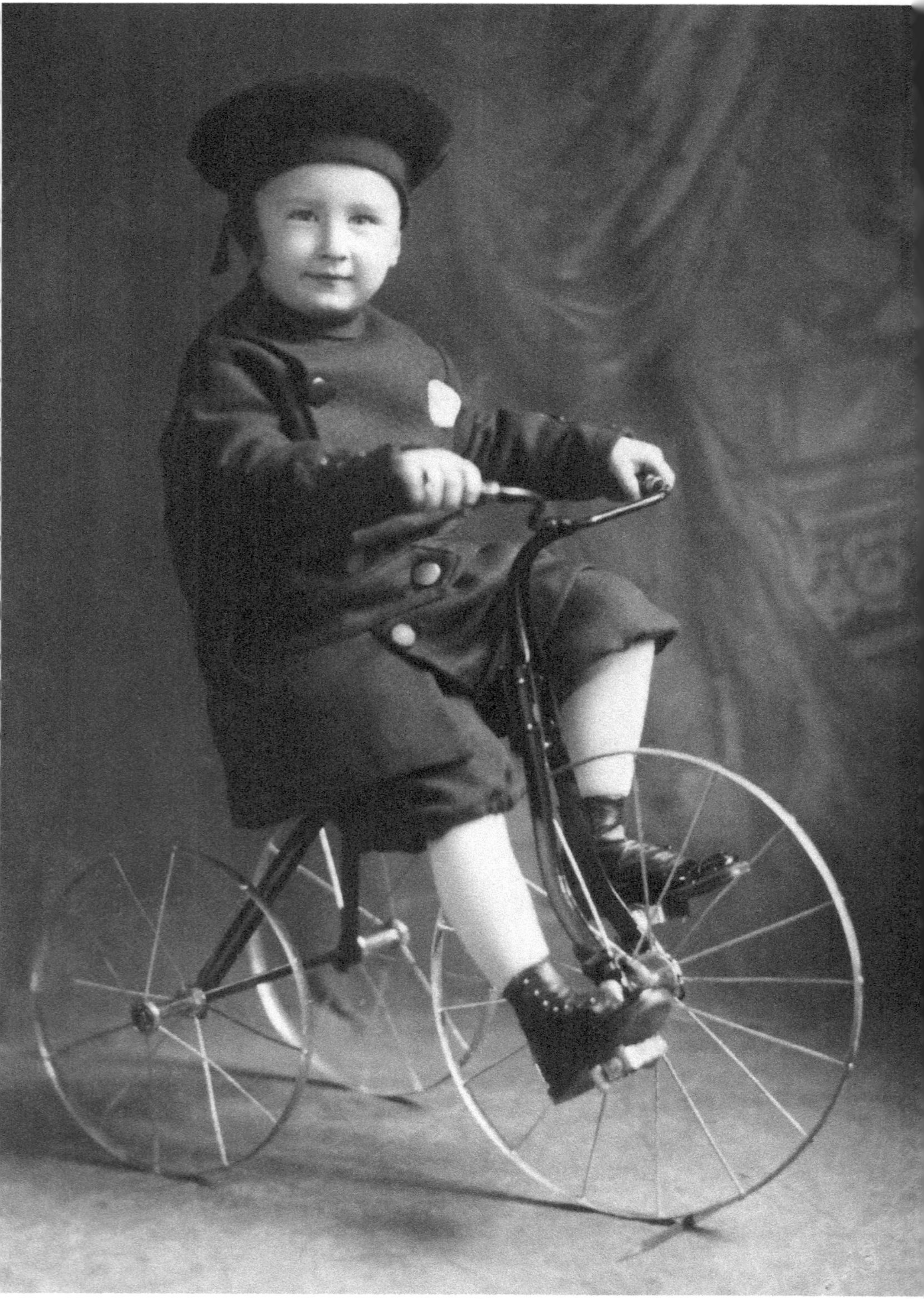

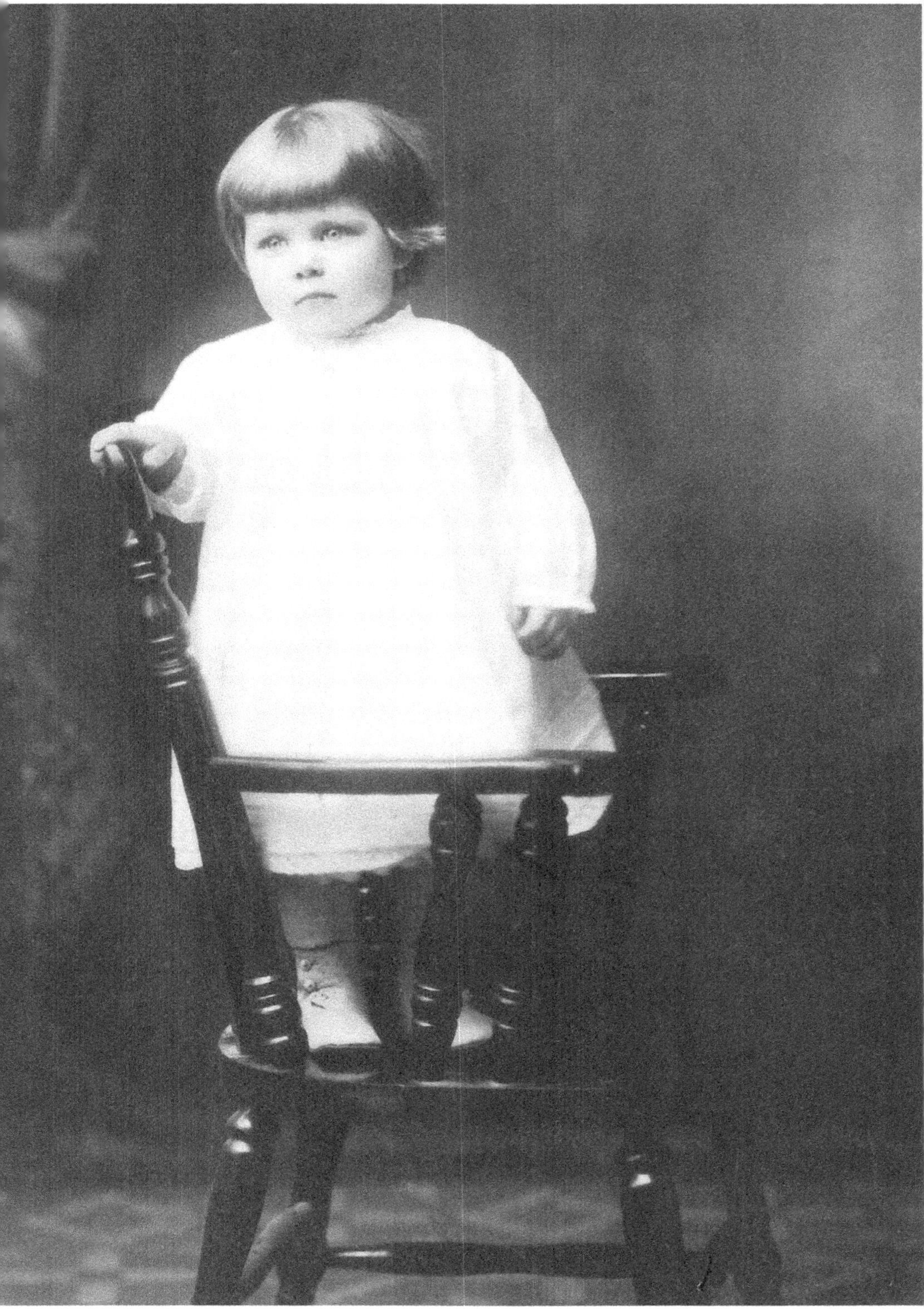

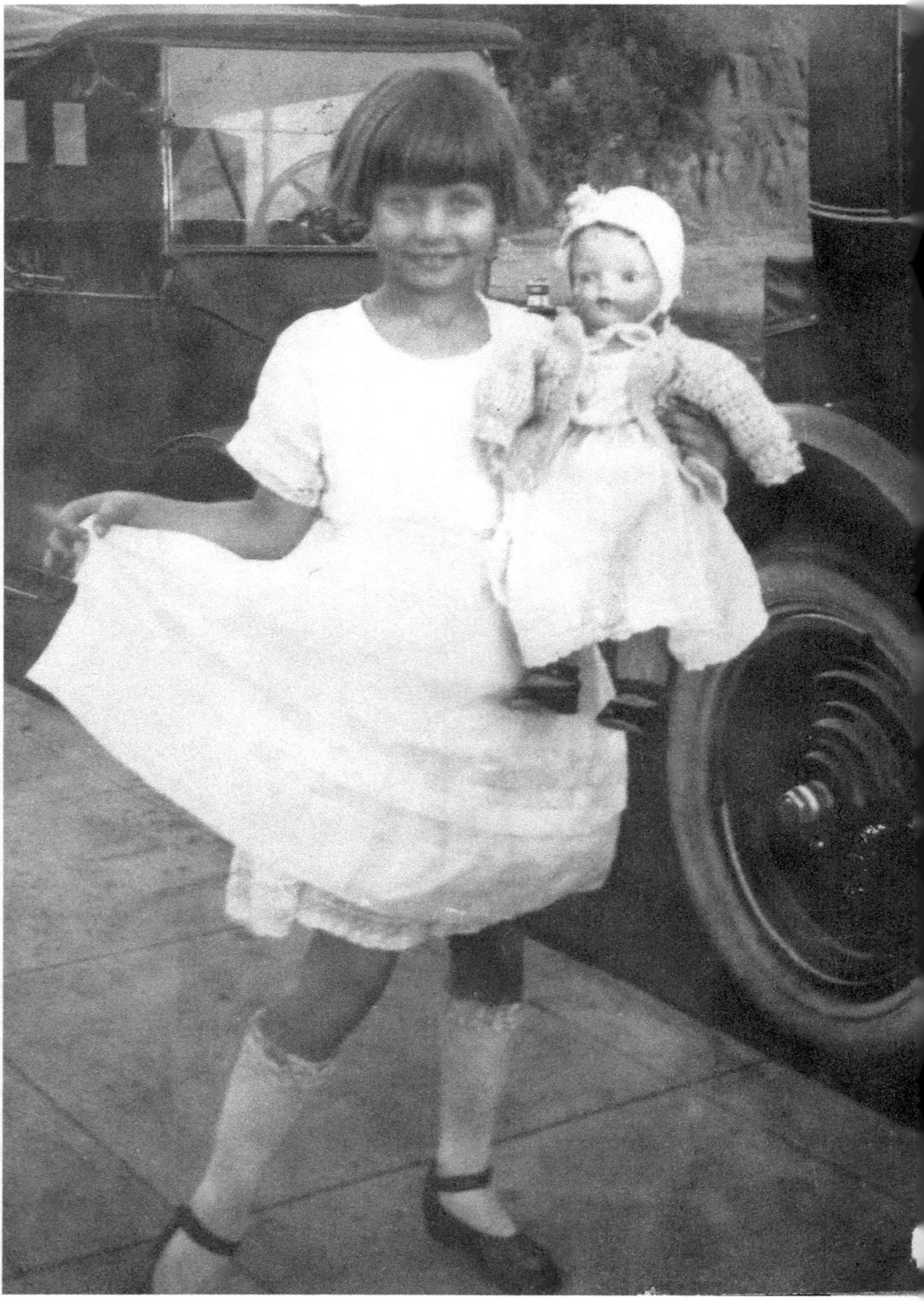

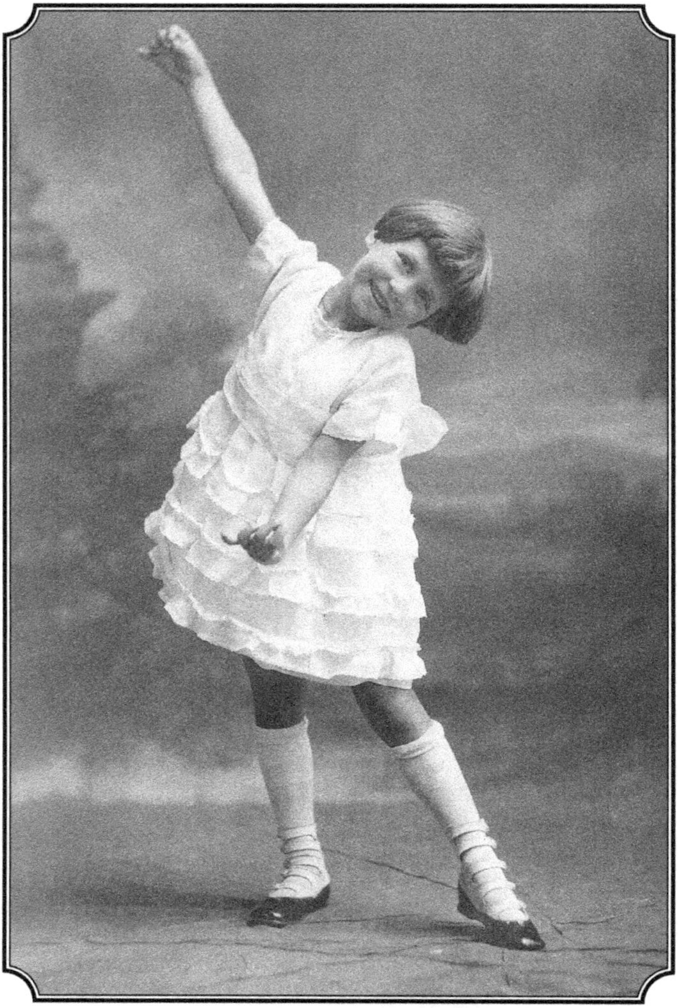

From the time I learned to write words, I liked to make them rhyme. At a very young age I created homemade birthday cards, much to the delight of my family, and I secretly yearned to become a writer someday. ❧ I was an eager reader as a child…spending hours devouring the classics, both poetry and prose. As I grew older I gradually fell under the spell of modern poets who wrote of love. ❧ By adolescence, I definitely had love on my mind. Too young for any participation, nothing could keep me from writing about it no matter how silly the poems were. From age ten I pestered my parents for dancing lessons. My old-fashioned grandma warned my mother, "That child wants to be a dancer so much she could wind up on the stage and even marry an actor!"

I took piano lessons!

Moon Signs

1925

Tonight
>The moon is a low-tipped glowing lantern
>Lit in the sky for a love-sign,
>Telling my love of the love-light
>Glowing in my heart for him.

Tonight
>The moon is a half-tipped flowing goblet
>Sparkling with potent love-wine,
>A toast tipped to him, awaiting his lips
>To drink love-wine from mine.

>O' God of sky and moon magic,
>Who has hung the moon-lantern and tipped the moon glass,
>Make him see the moon signs
>Set out for him
Tonight.

Spring Night

1928

The smooth full moon with rounded face
Has climbed the sky with singing grace
And smiles at me inscrutably—
With silver fingers pulls the sea
Into tides of whitened gold
And makes the sands a metal mold.

The flowers, born of a god who loves,
Perfume to sleep the mild-white doves,
And a strange bird belts out a trill
That seems to make the night more still.

And over all, my heart's quiet beat
Pulses with beauty—this night so complete
Has brought to a thirsty soul like mine
A quenching by moon and melody wine. ᕗ

You took my springtime and made it an early fall.

You pulled down the roses and showed me a barren wall.

You drew the silken curtain and I didn't like the view.

You were my first and most famous, I learned about

men from you!

I wasn't even dating yet!

To Mother and Leonard,
Yours,
Bud.

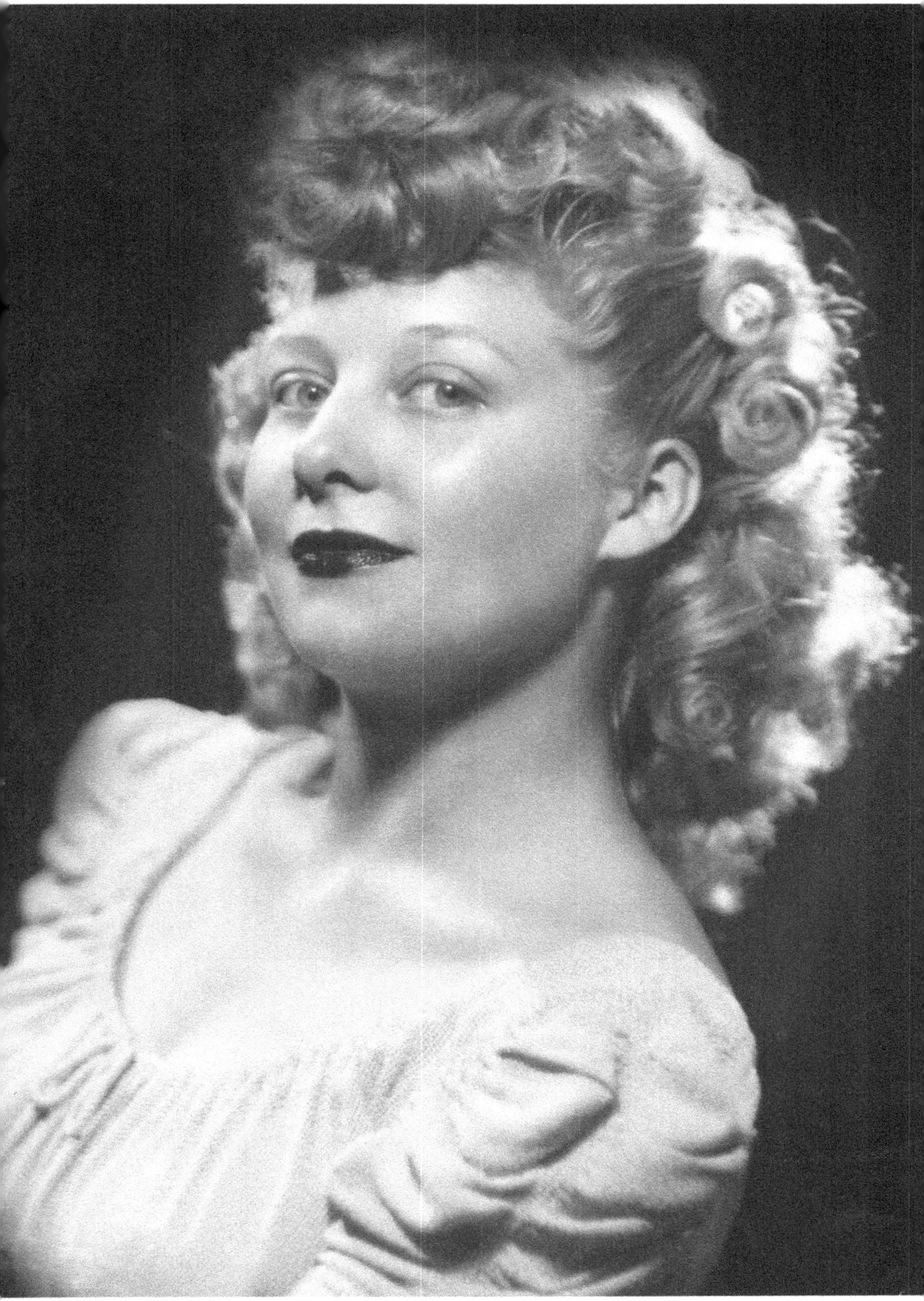

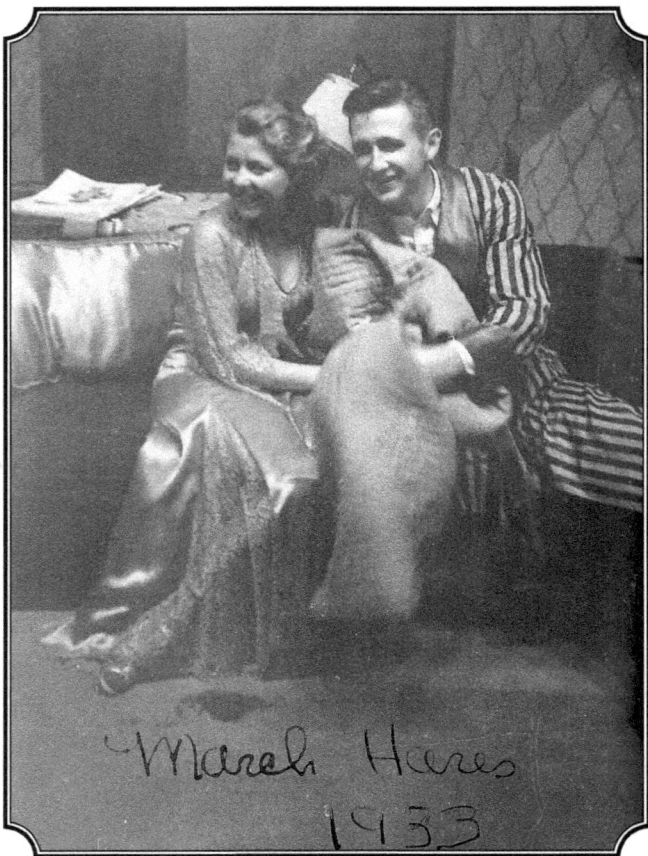

March Here
1933

As a freshman in college I joined the University Dramatic Society, and surprisingly found myself cast in a small part for their current production. Little did I know that the leading man, Lloyd Bridges, would fill that role in my life for the next sixty-odd years. ❧ One morning I received a rather cryptic, provocative Valentine. It was unsigned, but something about the sentiment, the cockiness and rashness of it, made me suspect who it was. Eventually he admitted it. I think I fell in love with him that night on our second date, as we sat in the rumble seat of his friend's car on our way home from a fraternity dance. It was cool and windy back there, so naturally he had to have his arm around me for protection. Then the first kiss happened and that one kiss lasted all the way to my house. I didn't want it to stop, ever. It seemed like he didn't want it to end either. Then we were at the door of my house. Another long kiss and then I watched from the window as he jumped the low hedge next to our driveway. "Wow!" he shouted to his friend as he got into the car. I felt suddenly faint as I looked in my dressing table mirror. "Wow!" I said. "This must be it, this must be love." ❧ A year later I wrote him a Valentine, the first one in a long succession. I suppose they could be considered a chronicle of life-long loving.

I know I should be studying
And writing a theme or two,
But how can I be studying,
And at the same time thinking of you?

I should be learning of outcrops,
Of deposits lain under the sea.
But the only "rock" I can think is the solitaire
That you might give to me.

I should be rehearsing my drama
And memorizing every cue.
The only speech I've memorized
Is the one I'll say to you.

Song of a CoEd
1935

I should be learning of nervous states
Or of functions of the brain.
The only psychological question I've asked
Is, "Can love drive one insane?"

There's a composition due in English
But I haven't found a theme.
The prof wouldn't like my one-track mind,
Or the title, "Love's Young Dream."

I should be studying the Renaissance
In the History of British Lit.
But instead I'm reviewing my love for you
And remembering the history of it.

Oh, I know I should be studying
And writing a theme or two.
But how can I be studying
And at the same time thinking of you?

So now I'll give up studying
And use this hour of mine
To start a life-long love poem
With this first Valentine. ✎

From the Desert
1938

The stillness I love,
And windy fronds whispering palm-words
Tamarisks understand and wave green fingers,
The sounds of palm-words
Blend with stillness.

Sand is still and white with its silence.
Smoke on the sunset hangs like cloud-dust.
A quail's soft flight over distant dunes
Leaves whirring muffled like a memory,
An eerie echoing of the stillness.

No sound could I bear here
But the thunder of your breath on my heart.

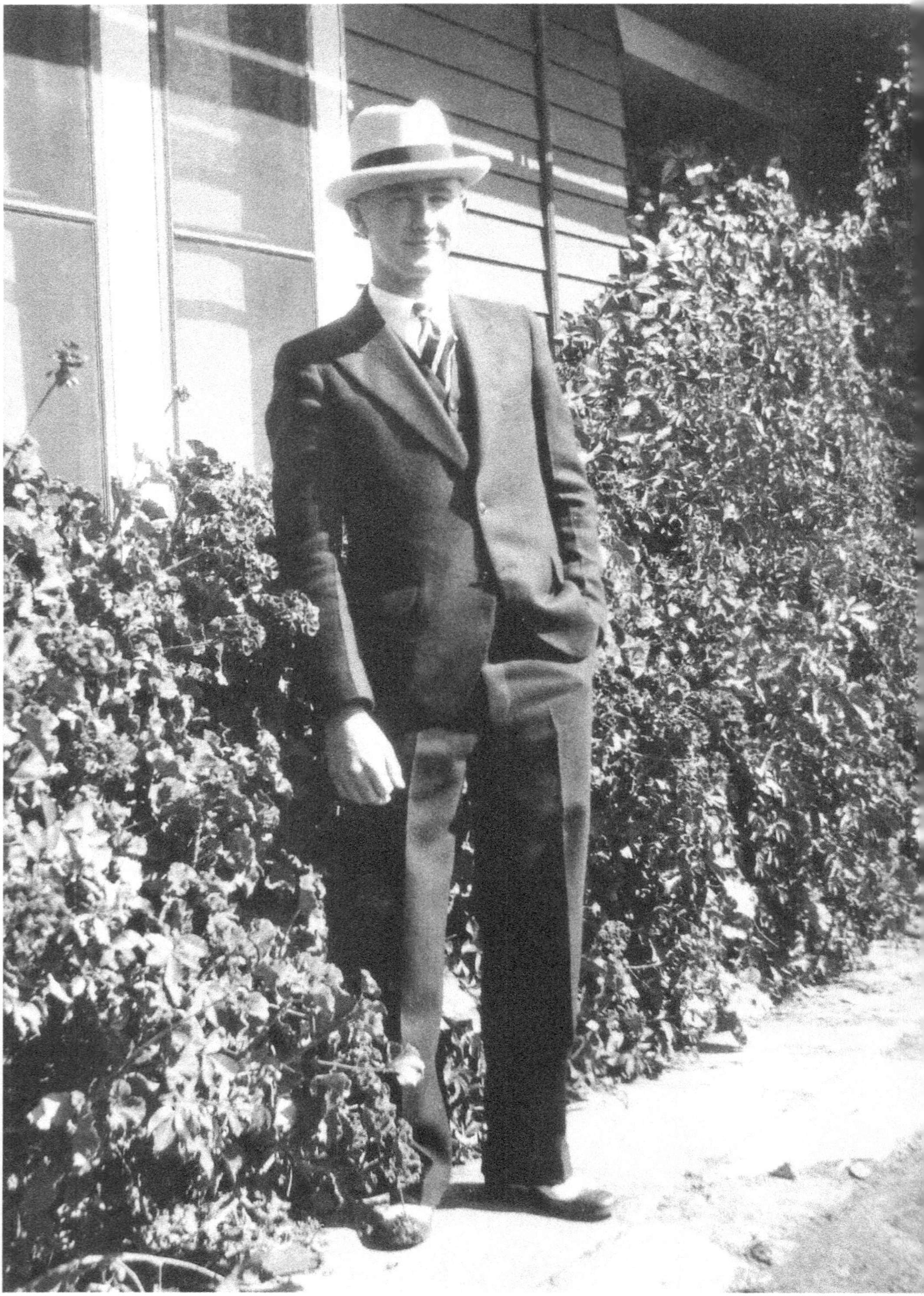

To L.V.B.

A year ago you sent a valentine
To an eager, dreamy girl.
And around that heart you sent her,
Her dreams began to whirl.
And she found that her dreams were true,
When the days let her discover
How fine, how true, how wonderful
Was her handsome, wilful lover.

And the dreams still are here,
And the heart is the same,
All built, all beating for you, dear.
And the girl wants to say
On Valentine's Day,
That she will ever be true, dear.

                    February 14, 1935

Suggestion

Let us have our love so glow
That only you and I will know
Flames that burn in either breast,
It matters little to the rest.
Only you and I should scheme
And make or break our little dream.
Keep each kiss and every sigh
Between just us —— the sea, the sky.

1935

Winter Song

1937

I wait for the strain of the wind to sunder
The web of my love, and I long for thunder
To drown my sweet singing. I seek the stinging
Of rain that will break and despair love's winging.

But this cold song is of winter's making. . .
Will its voice stop when the ice is breaking?
When the frost drops fast from the warmth of the tree
Will the spring chase these chill thoughts from me?

But now is the time that my heart starts singing
So faintly, but surely, I see the sign.
I leave all my doubting, I pick up my pen
To write you my usual Valentine.

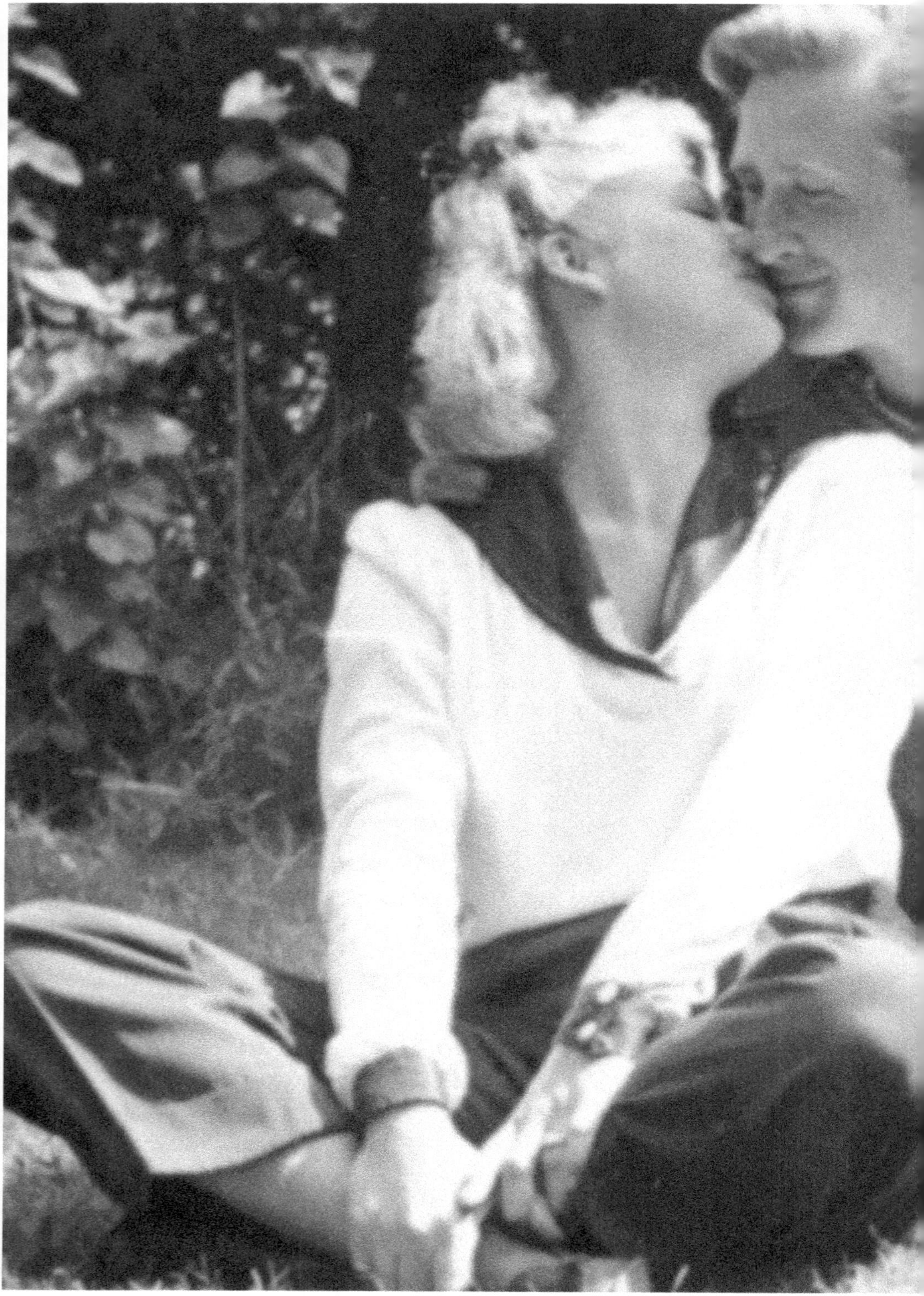

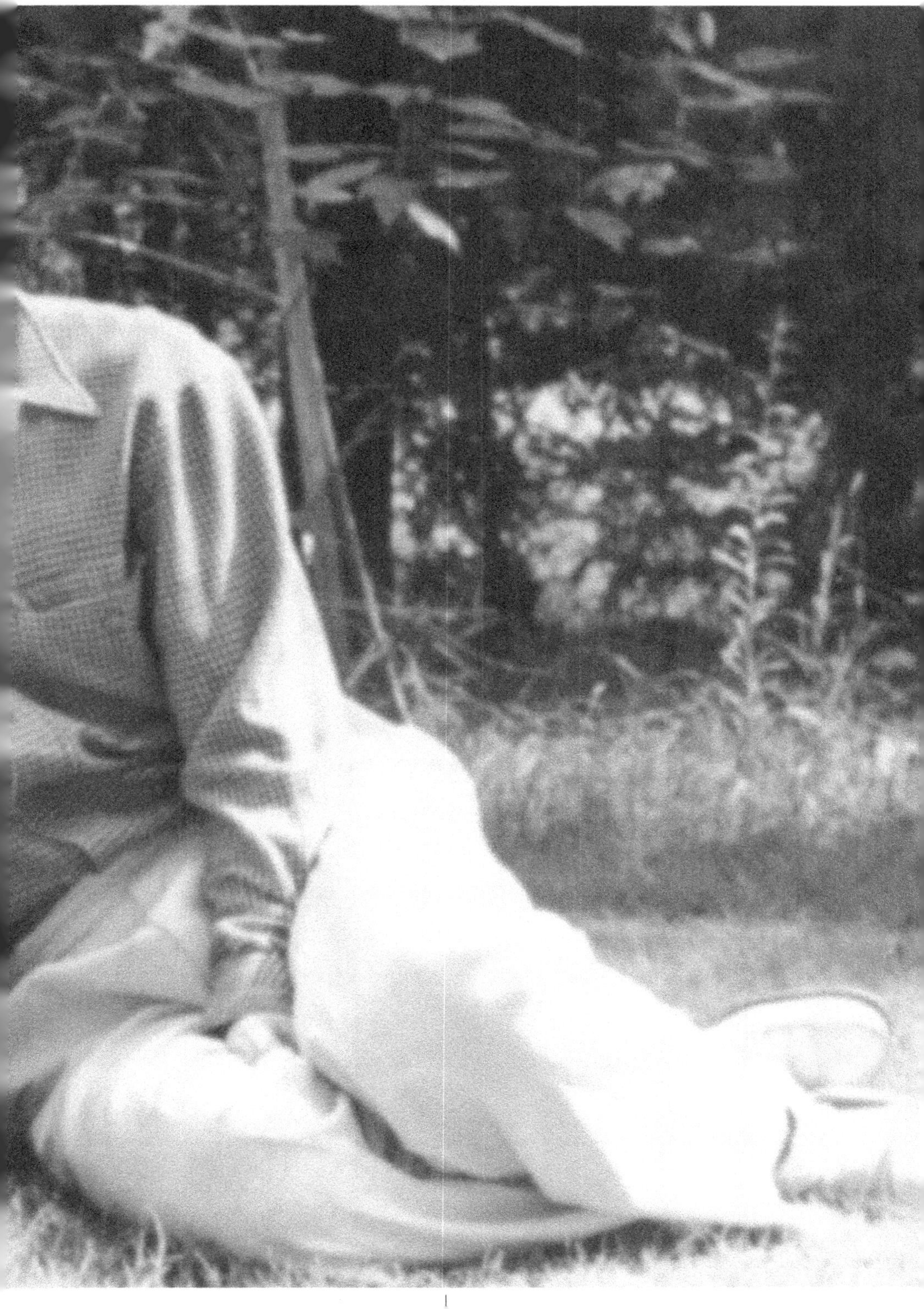

Just before he graduated from U.C.L.A., Lloyd told me he decided to become a professional actor and was going to New York to seek a future in the theater. "You ought to know," he said, "I don't think I should ever marry or anything like that. I'd like to feel as free as a gypsy, without promises or responsibilities to hold me back." ❧

Of course I was crushed, but for the first year of separation we had a passionate correspondence. Then the letters came less often, and I began to sense I wasn't the only girl in his life. Two years later I graduated and was trying to get him out of my heart and learning there was a possibility for me to have a less one-sided love affair with someone else. ❧

Suddenly he called from San Francisco to say he was visiting his mother and would I meet him there. Something made me say I would. At first we were very shy with one another. We'd been apart for a long time. After dinner with his family we went hand-in-hand for a walk in the warm dark night. ❧ Without warning he roughly pushed me against the broad trunk of a sycamore tree and kissed me with all the passion that had been banked up from our two years apart. I swear I heard a thousand violins playing. My God, I thought, we're still in love. ❧ "I guess we better get hitched," Lloyd said. It didn't seem like a very romantic proposal, and my father wasn't thrilled with the idea that he had asked for my hand. "You haven't much to offer my daughter," Daddy said. "No money, no job, no prospects. What are you going to live on?" ❧ There was no answer to that question, but Lloyd did sign a contract to make recordings for the *American Foundation for the Blind*, guaranteeing him seventy-two dollars a month. I knew I wasn't marrying a financial genius when he took a three-year lease on an apartment that cost seventy-five dollars a month. ❧ But hey, we couldn't have been any happier even if we had been rich.

Pre-Nuptial

1938

Now that the road is stretching before us,
Filled with mirage, with mire, and with winding,
Let's have the vows we take remain binding,
Keeping those dreams we'll need to restore us.
High is the road, and narrow in places.
Cliffs shear down sharply, ugly and warning.
Let us start out in clearness of morning,
With faith in our hearts and joy on our faces.

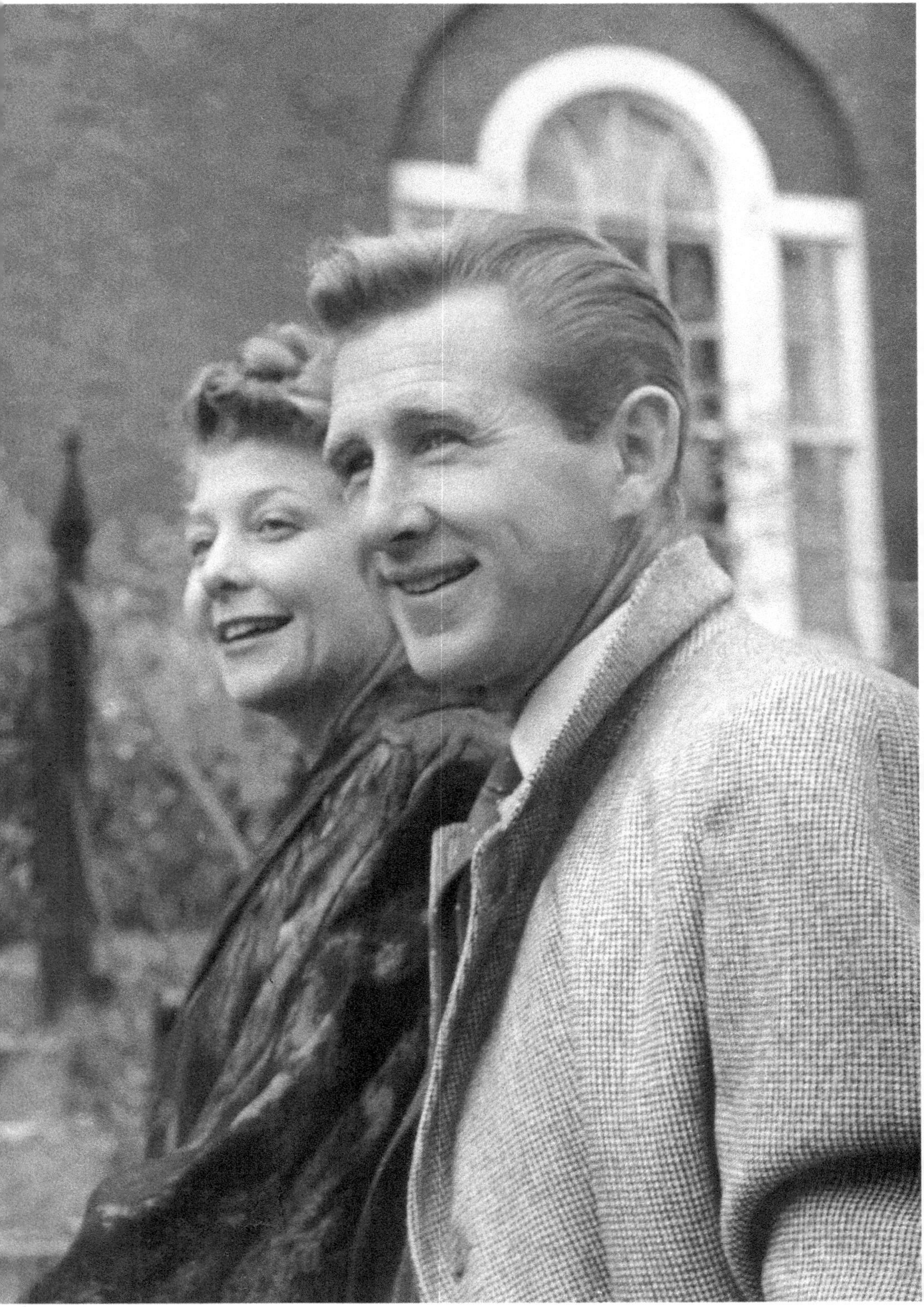

Not all the songs have yet been sung
Nor all the words yet written
Since I first joined my life with yours,
With you, my love, been smitten.
Another chapter's just begun,
Will challenge and will bless us,
So let's be brave, and thankful, too,
Not tide nor time impress us.
My poems rain down like autumn leaves
Redundantly above you,
And all of them say just one thing,

"I love you,

love you,

love you!"

A Valentine is more to me
Than just a red frivolity—
A satin heart, a tinseled sweet
Are empty symbols, incomplete.
A Valentine is when you rise
To hush-a-bye the baby's cries.
A Valentine is when you phone
And say, "Hi, Ma, what's new at home?"
A Valentine is when you shout,
"Take off that apron, let's eat out!"
A Valentine is when we kiss,
Or talk at home one hour unharried.
My Valentine I say is this—
The great big joy of being married.

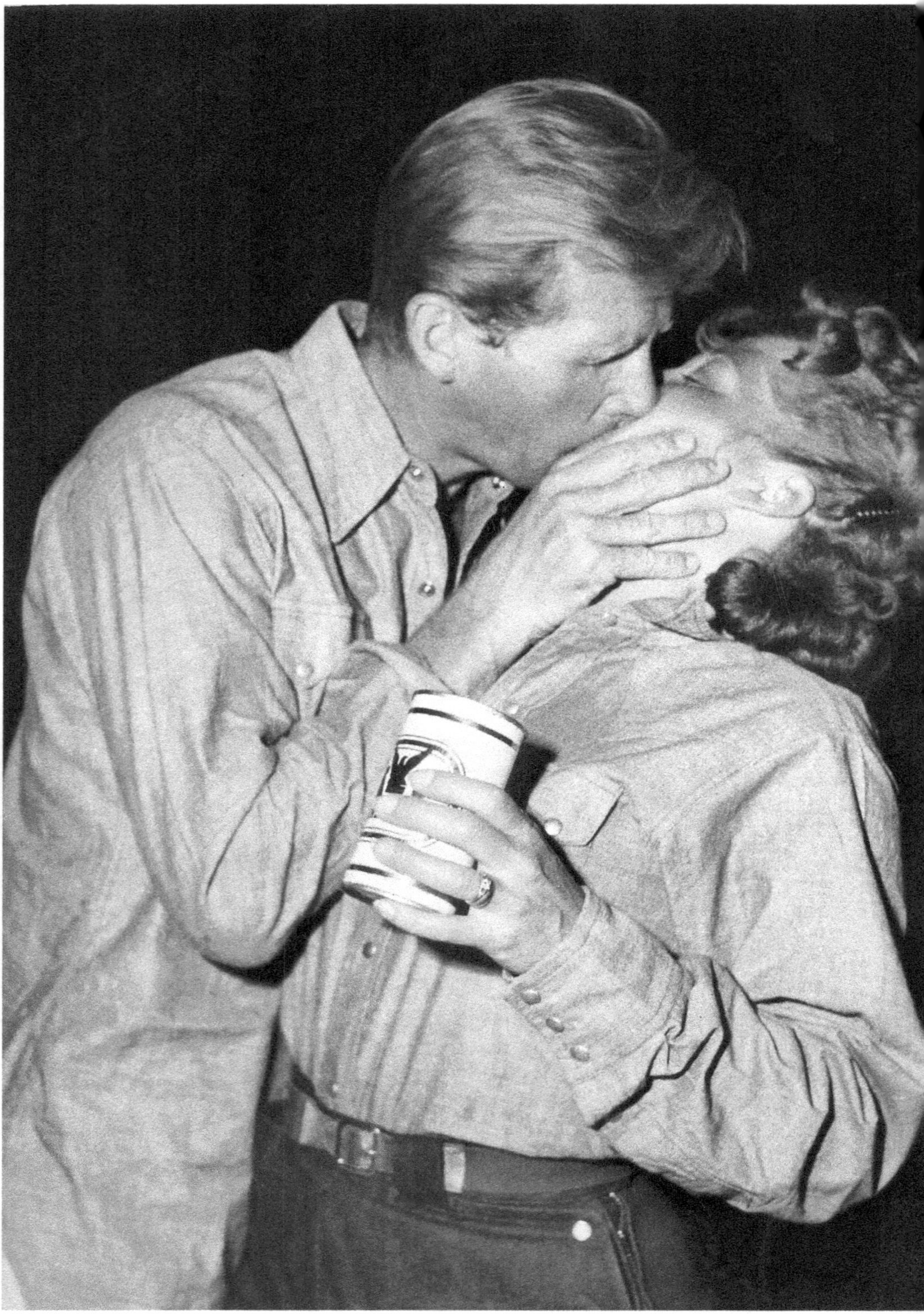

Valentine to a Married Man

1956

The years have left most favorably their mark
And altered only for the best your charms.
The warming still is there within your arms,
Now from a fire that started as a spark.
The boy once loath to just but plight his troth
Is now both faithful husband and a sire.
You put the cans out, lay the evening fire.
Your tamed free hand now feeds the baby broth.
O' Husband, do not rue the years that bind
Your past and present closely up with mine.
It could be worse, and better still we'll find
The fruit that lingers yet upon the vine.
When first you sent a heart your fate was signed,
That day I chose for good my Valentine.

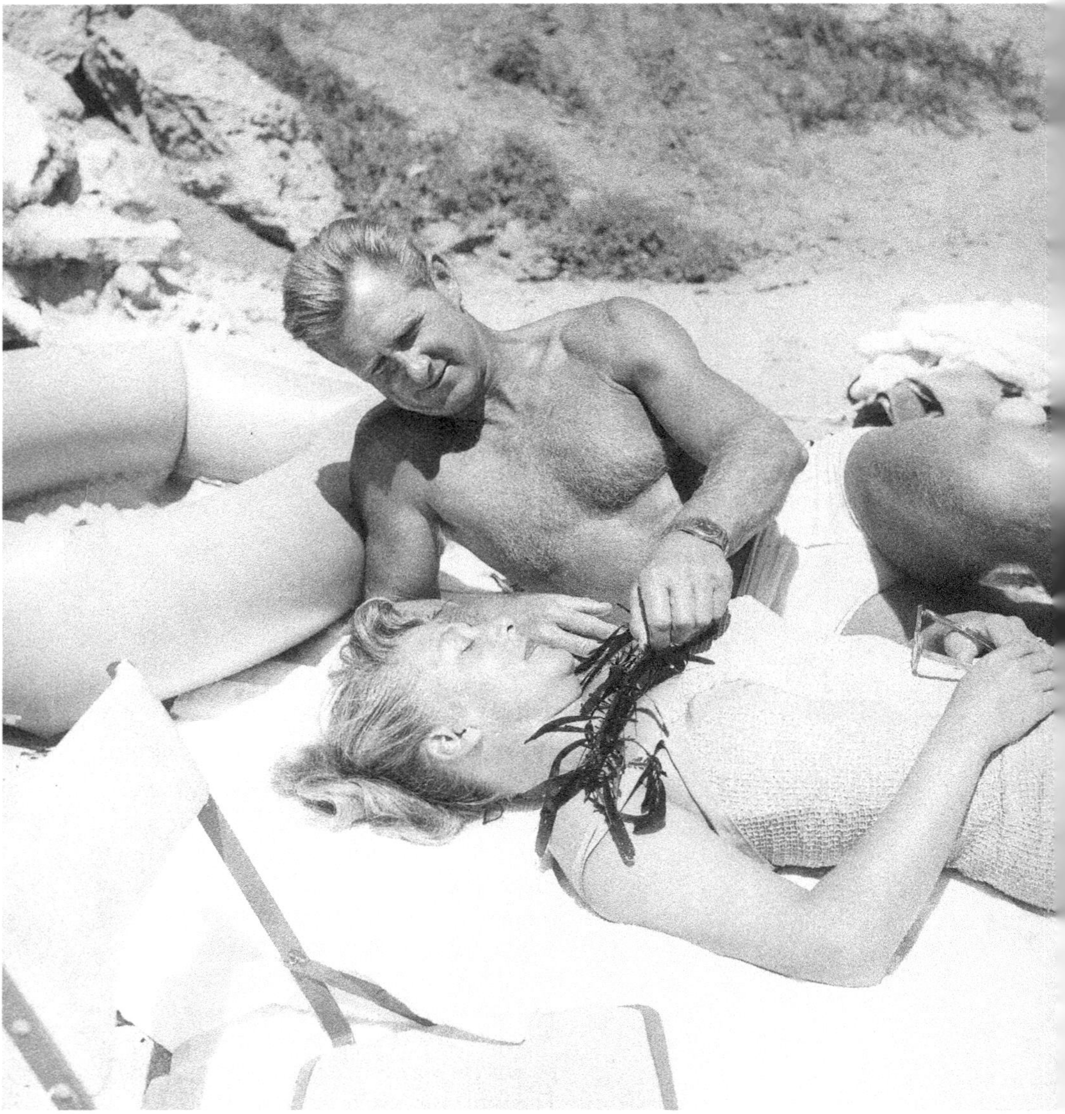

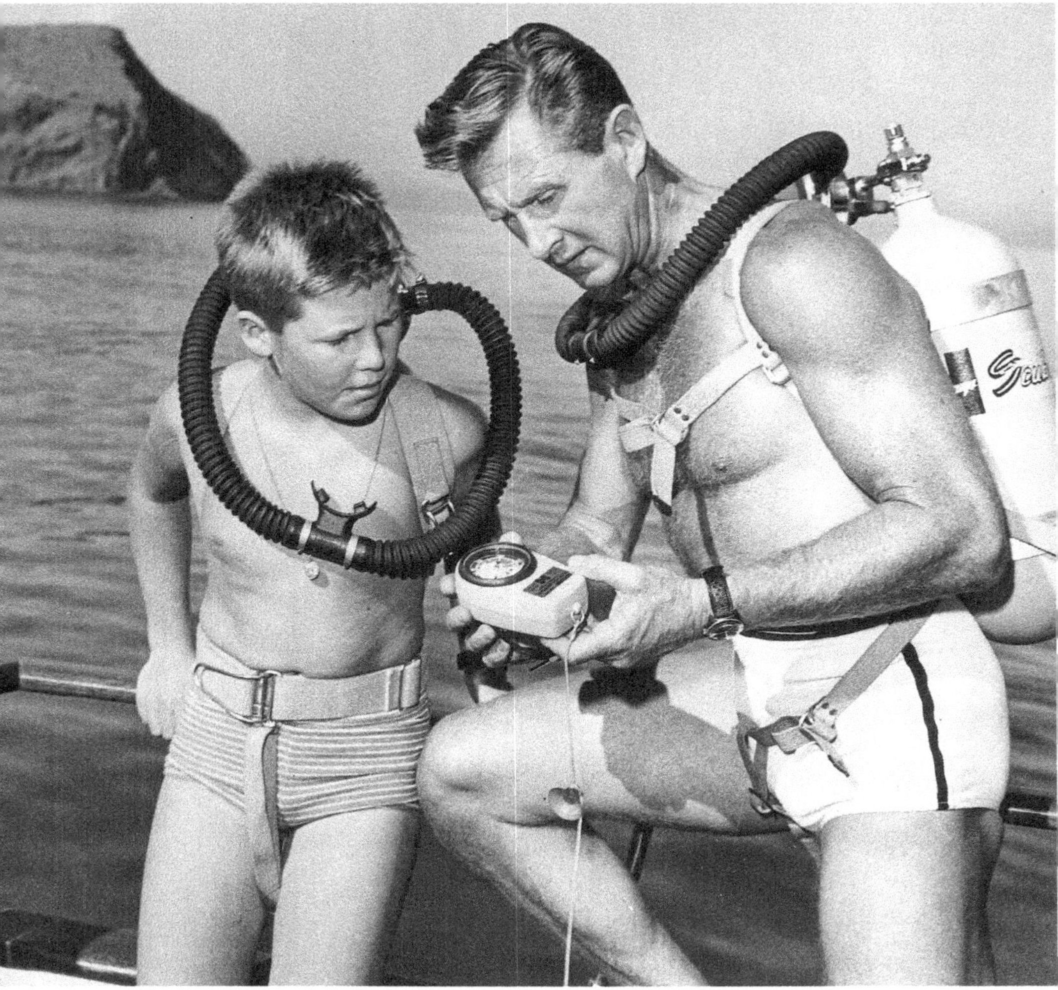

Now once again here's true love's sign,
Our two hearts joined, a Valentine,
And that's the way it's been with you,
Romancing all the short years through.
So thank you husband, king of hearts,
For shooting me with cupid's darts.
You hit the jackpot thrice I know,
For there are

Cindy,
Jeff, &
Beau!

On this sweet day I live to tell my love
the story, oft retold, of our romance,
And how it had been writ in stars above
that he and I met at that college dance.
By now, made so redundant through the ye
the saga of our youthful passion bores
those husband-like, yet dear and patient ear
Accustomed also to my wails and roars!

But sweet, just harken, and you'll be surprise
A whole new chapter's added to the tale —
I love you more than ever you've surmised,
Am sure now love can weather any gale!

When young, I thought: "I'll get him if I can!"
Today I say with pride: "this is my man

Take my heart
—its yours

whata yer gonna do?,

Except love!

Your wife
2/14/63

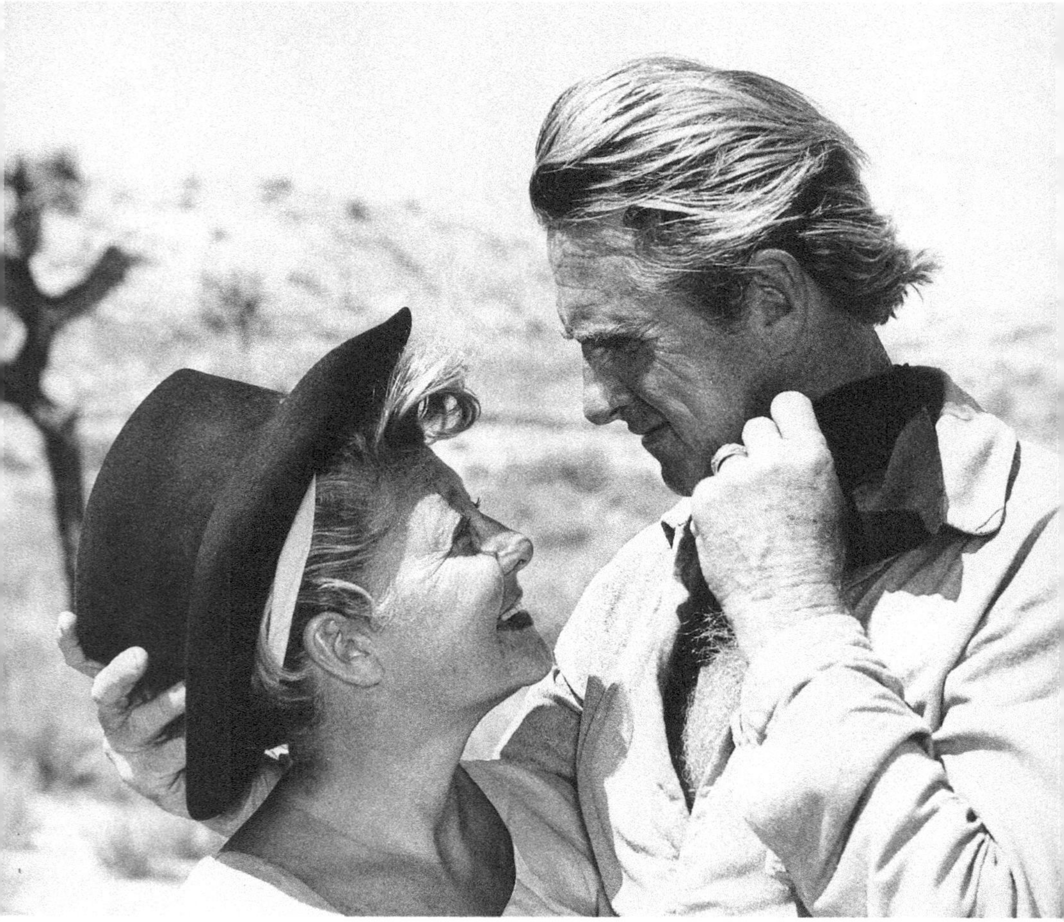

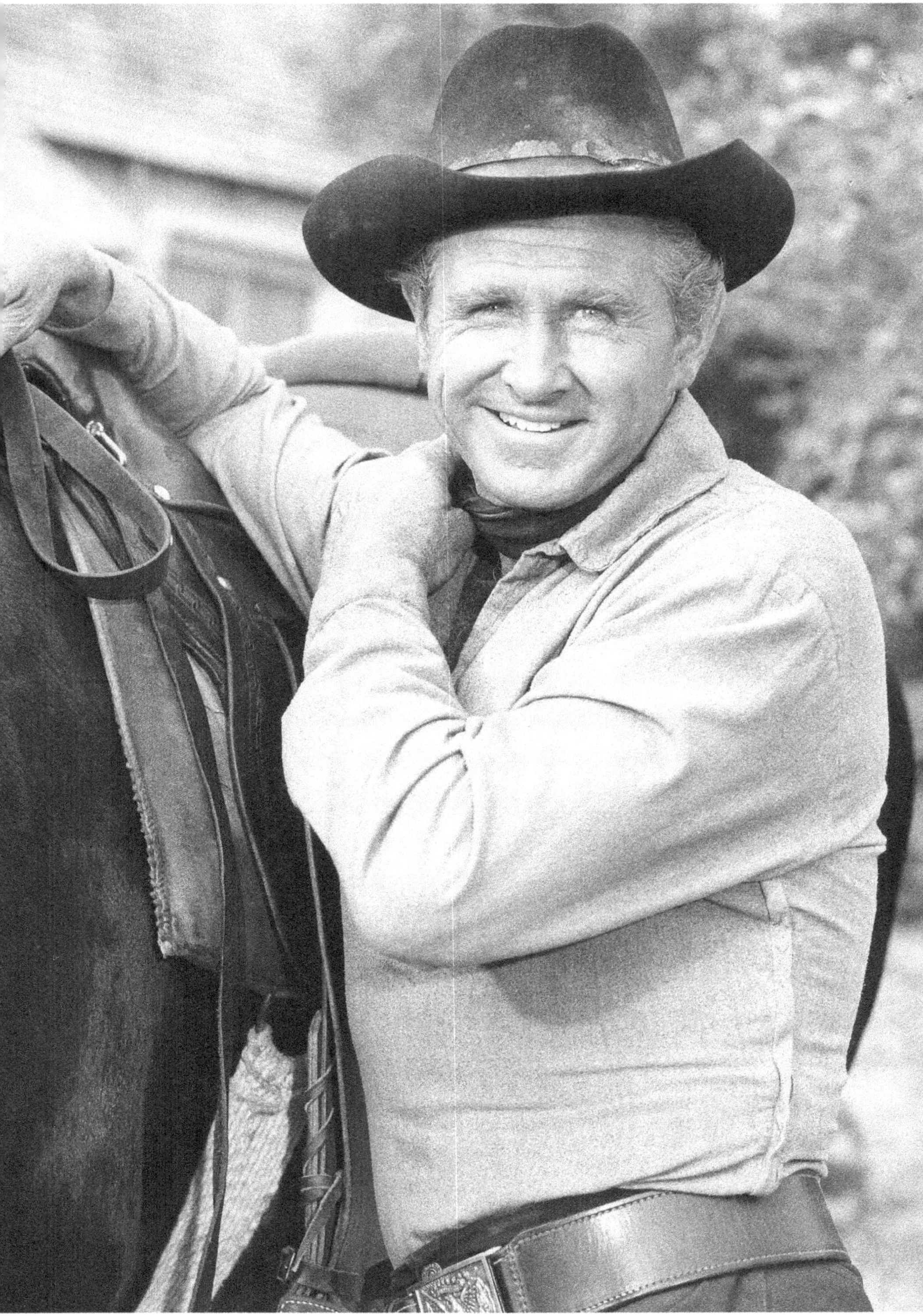

Our love is still in bloom—
The living goes just fine.
Though winter could be near,
There's fruit upon the vine.
And so my darling man,
My heart's still on the line
And life has proved I must
Keep you my Valentine. ⬱

'DOROTHY and LLOYD'

Anniversary

1972

How brave we were, how brave and young.
Those many, many years ago
As heart to heart we pledged our troth,
Then faced a winter world of snow.
A world where work and hope were scarce,
And doubt beclouded everything.
How grateful, we, for young love's warmth
That kept us safe until the spring.
How gay we were, how fair and fine,
When summer saw us stretch and grow,
While fortune's smile was warm on us,
Three children quickened life's sweet flow.
There were times we felt the chill
Of dear ones lost, of love lain low.
But somehow though, we struggled on
To reach this autumn and its glow.
How rich we are, how wise to know
That we two halves can be one whole
And share within our universe
All varied seasons of the soul.
Now hand in hand we can walk tall
To face the future free from fear.
When I have you and you have me
It matters not what time of year.

S lowly but surely my husband's career took off. When he created the role of Mike Nelson in the TV series, *Sea Hunt*, he became a certifiable television star, known and admired throughout the world. By then his movie career was blossoming too, and we were finally financially secure. As our homes became more impressive, so did our growing family with the additions of Beau, Jeff, and Lucinda. There were challenges along the way: the loss of our baby boy Garry from a crib death, the near ruin of Lloyd's career by the shameful Un-American Activities Committee, and my husband's occasional infidelities. ❦ Did we separate? No! Somehow I knew, as I had many years before, that he was a man worth waiting for, and he was smart enough to realize he didn't want to risk losing what meant more to him than anything else in his life. ❦ The marriage lasted for sixty years and the Valentines were written every year of that marriage, no matter how stressed were the marital bonds or how blissful the long periods of unforgettable happiness. ❦ The Valentines never stopped, and all together they tell the story.

February 14, 1975

Valentines are silly
And Valentines are solly
And often known to be a lot of riot—
Though my dear love's a dilly
I'll keep him, willy-nilly,
For he's the only Valentine
I got!

and I loves him!

Valentines are frilly

And Valentines are silly

And often known to be a lot of rot—

Though my dear love's a dilly

I'll keep him, willy-nilly,

For he's the only Valentine I got!

1975

The heart can break most noisily,
The pieces clanging as they scatter,
Or sometimes crack so silently
One scarcely hears the final patter.

On Our Thirty-Seventh

Be this our symbol of the chain that binds
Our lives together—carefully made of gold,
But magic stuff, with power to change all kinds
Of darkness into light, to warm the cold.

The links could be the years that march so fast,
That dashed through spring and summer, now in fall
Remind us of the richness of our past,
That winter isn't far away at all.

And let the clasp be ever-loving arms
Encircling, keeping safe the loving way we know,
Protecting one another from life's harms,
Yet opening when we feel it's time to go. . .

October 14, 1975

1977

So very much has happened
Since we first loved, we two;
The ups, the downs, the doldrums,
What stages we've been through!
Thus can we wax romantic
As when our love began?

I'm here to tell you, darling,
You bet your ass we can.

Now must we still be counting?
The score has run up high,
And I became a grandma
And you're an older guy.
Why can't we push a button
That takes us way back when
You bulged with sexy muscles,
I was a cute size ten?
The answer comes most clearly,
It always is a shock,
No matter how one tries it
You sure can't stop the clock.
And if we would be happy
The smartest thing by far
Is just to go on loving
Whatever way we are!

Happy Valentine's Day!
I'm not very good with poetry.
And I've never been quite sure just
what blank verse is. So... You're going
to have to settle for these simple words,
"I love you." And I love you for
so many things. At the top of the list, of
course are our 3 wonderful, beautiful,
talented kids. I love you for your
faith in me and the support you've given
me thru-out the years. I love you INFINITY!
Yours.

Handwritten valentine from my husband, 1980

1980

How many Valentines? I've now lost count
Of those you sent to me and I to you.
I know the years have piled up quite a mount
Of memories—the living we've been through!
I see the frilly time, all lace and gold,
When Cupid smiled and words were poetry.
Remember, too, the days when love grew cold—
(The only arrows shot went right through me!)
The funny Valentines, and ones you made;
That sexy first one sent without your name—
They've all been saved—where time can never fade
That shining source of love from which they came.
By God, it looks as though true love can win—
So have those Valentines keep coming in!! ✎

1981

We are not always lovers,
And if the truth we should tell,
Sometimes I send you poison darts,
You have made me mad as hell.
So long have we known each other
That faults are clear to see.
I've had to give up changing you,
And for sure you are stuck with me.
The left-over dirt from the bad days
Is swept clear under the rug,
Forgiveness is what's between us now
In a heavy duty hug.
The champagne of youth was heady,
Today we're sipping still wine,
But dammit all, there still lives love
And won't you be my Valentine? ⬎

1982

When we consider all the years we've spent
Devoted to our love's demanding rule,
I say, "How fast the spring and summer went!"
I wonder how we each have kept our "cool."
I worry should the future be less kind,
And if I ever left you, would you mind
That there were no Valentines one day?
Thank God, with age there comes a stoic heart,
It knows we cannot count on what will be.
An optimistic outlook must be part
Of any future time for you and me.
So Valentine, we now can understand
That all goes well when we go hand-in-hand!

1983

Once more, dear love, across the miles I fly
To that sweet place I know my heart will be.
Impatiently I sail the endless sky
To where a special joy is there for me.
The hours away, the days so empty spent
Were needed, I suppose, to show us how
We often took for granted love's event,
How grateful that we have it now.
They say it's wise to spend some time apart,
That marriage often needs a breathing space,
But once I'm in it, then for sure I start
To miss the one I love, his voice, his face.
I sense your arms outstretched, is this a sign
You need me, too, to be your Valentine?

1984

The lacy frills, red satin bows,
The box of candy hearts.
The cards of sentimental verse,
The golden cupid darts—
These are the bright gay tokens, love,
Of every lover's sign
To make this day romantic, but
There's more, my Valentine!
To us who've spent a million hours
In our true love's delight,
But also shared the morning's toil,
The terrors of the night;
To us who know what winning is,
The sorrow of great loss;
Who understand some "giving in,"
And what it's like to boss;
To us who find contentment still
In keeping side by side,
Who in our children have such joy
And monumental pride,
To us who live together, love,
And find the living fine—
Then life itself will ever be
One great big Valentine. ✍

To My Love on Valentine's Day in New York

1985

How right it is that we are here,
Where married Valentine began.
'Twas here we made the pact, my love,
Endowed with such a dream, a plan.
We walked these canyons' hard cement
And hurried down the teeming street
To find the comfort of our hearth—
And it was always there, my sweet.
Today it's quite a different tale,
The fame and fortune have been won,
The struggle's over, all we need
Is time and strength to have the fun.
But hotel suites, the limousines—
That's just the frosting on the cake.
Wherever you are that's my life
And that's the Valentine you make.

1986

"How's about it, Valentine?"
 My husband, does that ring a bell?
 Yes, you sent it years ago
 And I was cast into love's spell.
"How's about it, Valentine?"
 What was on your mind to say,
 Were you asking for a date,
 A kiss, a roll in the good old hay?
 No, you didn't sign your name,
 But somehow I just guessed and knew
 No one else could be so fresh,
 The boldness made me sure 'twas you.
 Though we share a lifelong love,
 Are we too weak to make a sign,
 No sparks left, but steady flame,
"How's about it, Valentine?"
 Will you take my crumpled hand
 And dance me, darling, down the line?
 Will love somehow keep us warm?
"How's about it, Valentine?"

1987

A truth on which couples can always rely—
The evidence is quite impartial—
The wandering "eye," like the wandering "i,"
Changes MARITAL state into

MARTIAL.

1989

Often love gets tougher with the years—
(Bloody footprints on the sands of time)
Trying hard means sweat, and sometimes tears—
Love songs get off-key and poems won't rhyme.
That's when lovers fail—or pass the test—
That's when lovers need some mystic sign—
That's when you and I will be our best
As once again we make a Valentine!

1991

When love goes on for such great length
It's hard to summon up the strength
It takes to let your lover know
Just how and why you love him so. . .
My head's grown empty, purpose weak,
The flowery words no longer speak,
And dimming eyes can seldom spark
The looks that used to hit the mark.
But darling, I can swear it's true,
That in my heart there's banked for you
A fire of love that's white with heat,
That makes this winter chill retreat.
And when you warm your lips on mine
You'll know you've found your Valentine!

On My Husband's Birthday

Don't count the years, my love, they do not show
The quality of how your life is spent.
Don't place false value on what mirrors know,
The beauty love reflects is truer meant.
Don't long for youthful times that used to be,
Or mourn the dreams that never did come true.
The past is best used as a memory,
And every day can build new dreams for you.
Don't thrust aside the honor of your age,
Nor make acceptance difficult and glum.
Relentless ticks the clock, despite your rage,
So live with pride in what you have become.
Dear heart, the love that fills our life so much
Creates a magic age that time can't touch.

January 15, 1995

Happy sailing!
Lloyd Bridges

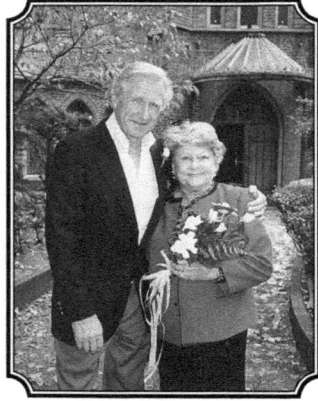

Fifty Years Later a Valentine

1988

Does love mean less when lovers have grown old?
Why can't the flowers bloom right through the snow?
Does lack of passion mean the hearts grew cold,
Are memories the only warmth we know?
The touches lose their urgency it seems,
And kisses lack that old seductive fire.
Is practicality a trade for dreams,
And "reason" now that trait we most admire?
There should be mystic ways that couples find
To nourish love, the rarest gift of life.
Was it the joy and lightness left behind
As we matured into a man and wife?
Let's look into soul's mirror, love, and see
The good, the beauty that we have today.
It isn't youth alone that makes love be.
Let time go shake "the darling buds of May,"
When I see you I take it for love's sign,
In Spring or Winter, you're my Valentine! ≈

1991

From Tokyo to Dublin
From Rio to high Machu Pichu
I've had the chance to love you,
To happily touch and to reach you,
For lo, these fifty-two years
From Monaco to London,
From Athens and island of Bali
In Leningrad and Sydney,
We've bedded, and then some, by golly,
And conquered lots of our fears.
From Aberdeen to Hong Kong,
Helsinki, and Paris, and Nandi,
I've toured with you, my darling,
And most of the trips were just dandy,
Our troubles only a few.
Now here we are in Bangkok,
Just recently come from Strathqarry.
I look at you with passion,
The man I decided to marry,
The one who loves me, too. . .
I thank the sun for shining
On most of the roads we have taken,
The stars whose promise led us
When sometimes our purpose was shaken.
I listen for songs yet unheard.
So pop champagne, dear husband,
Let's celebrate while we're still able—
Let's dance the light fantastic,
Let's pull up our chairs to the table
And

Toast to our Fifty-Third ⁌

1991

You are everything to me—
The good, the bad, the in-between,
Past and present, what's to be;
My world, and inner space unseen.
Have I ever wished undone
The bindings that my love has wrought;
Rued the day that made us one,
Or wondered if it's all for naught?
Ask me not, but rather guess
From day to day my state of mind.
Even if the answer's "yes,"
More loyal wife you'll never find.
What I am is yours—and mine
Is such as you for Valentine.

1992

The paper lace is fragile now,
The hearts red fire grows fainter, too,
But we are here to note the day,
Though not the way we used to do.
The look of love in tired eyes,
And words of love so slow and weak,
Can mean much more to each of us
Than presently we see or speak
Our history of love is long,
Through tears we've learned the sun will shine,
And here's my yearly promise, love,
You'll always be my Valentine.

1993

Where are those two of yesteryear,
He with the muscles out to here,
She of the figure shaped just right,
Could they have disappeared from sight?

Where is that actor on the make,
Expecting to give the world a shake?
Where's the young wife and mommy, too,
Did they slip away before we knew?

Where went the action, the kissing and bedding,
Keeping them warm when there was such tough sledding?
Where is the tennis, the skiing, the dancing?
And is it true they're no longer prancing?

Yes, there've been changes hard to make,
Lessons to learn, some tough to take.
Fate has been kind though, through it all,
Left them still standing proud and tall.
Counting the blessings new and old,
Treasures of life more rich than gold,
Fitting together like hand in glove.

yes, they're still here,
& still in love!

Portrait of My Husband at Malibu

1994

It is six o'clock.
He is sitting on the deck,
His profile against the sea.
The last sun rays bathe him,
A brisk wind ruffles his fine grey-gold hair.
There is a sadness and peace in his repose.
His eyes shut.
The jaw blurred and slightly slack.
A deep laugh line etched on the side of his lean cheek continues
Under his chin and up the other side of his face.
His body is hard, showing little wear for its years of service,
Only the soul shining from his still very blue eyes is old and tired, unsmiling.

Tears well in my eyes.
There sits my dream of love, my hero,
The one I was young with. . .
There he sits in the sunset of our life.

To My Husband

Is this a marriage made in heaven?
My God, the years count 57!
So think about the past we've shared
The times well spent, the things we dared.

Is this the marriage, for example,
Of perfect love. . .Is this the sample?
Oh no, we two must now admit
There've been some things quite wrong with it.

Is this the marriage we're well-stuck with,
The union we've had lots of luck with?
By now, sweet love, we should have guessed
Life blessed us both. . .

We've got the best!

On My Darling's Birthday

1996

Can we believe it, can it be
My college boy is eighty-three?
Though everything is said and done
I think you still as twenty-one.
So handsome, such a lusty stud
A girl could dance for hours with Bud,
And yet be ready to retreat
For romance in the rumble seat.

I think of all the happy times
We counted nickels and our dimes.
Those first years of our wedded bliss
We had a million dollar kiss.

Remember with me glory hours
Just when it seemed the world was ours.
The kids, the jobs, the money came
And everywhere they knew your name.
Yes, there were sorrows for us, too,
But we survived, we made it through.

We now continue at the feast,
Fly north and south and west and east.
We're walking slower, dancing less,
And missing out on stuff, I guess.
Your bride of eighty knows it's true
Her life begins and ends with you,
So fill the glass and cut the cake
And let us these thanksgivings make.
Our luck and love could only be
Because you're here at eighty-three!

1997

The memories come crowding
Of each absorbing year,
The challenges, the blessings,
And love stood always near.
It's simply overwhelming,
How can we know it's true,
For fifty-nine sweet years, Bud,
Our married joys just grew.

Now are the days more scary,
Diminished most our joys,
And we grow more dependent
Upon our girls and boys.
Is patience often lacking,
Is walking just a chore?
And aren't we two just greedy
For wanting so much more?

The eighties can't be easy,
We naturally feel sad
When family picture albums
Reveal what we once had.
The calendar seems somber,
The future years too few
To cram in all those wonders
That we once hoped to do.

But darling, there's still magic,
We somehow must believe,
And take more time for loving,
Less time to sigh and grieve.
We'll note there's lots of living
Left in our well-used cup
If we be bold and daring
To sip that living up.

See in my eyes the love light
That through our life endures,
And I will know the special
Sweet look I see in yours.
Take hold my hand forever,
Your hand belongs in mine.
We'll slowly walk together
The journey will be fine.
And adds to our collection
Another Valentine. ⤵

Bud
Loves
Dorothy

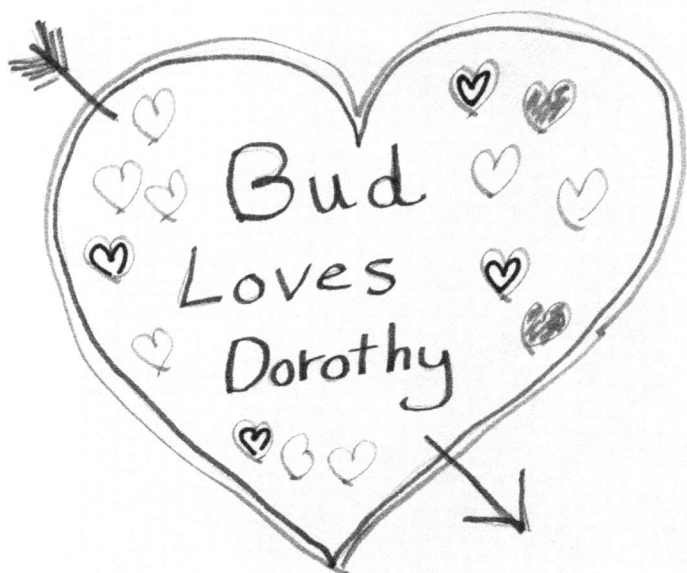

I Love you,
Your Husband

Valentine's Day '98
(made by Sean)

He was hardly ever sick. I was the weaker one. It didn't seem right when the day came for me to take care of him. ❧ I could accept old age, even if I didn't like it, but trying to endure the fact that someday we could be apart forever was another thing. ❧ After that sad day he died I was sorting through things he left behind. There in an old cardboard box were the Valentines and other love poems, for us a precious history of our love. ❧ Could I suddenly stop loving him so much? Could I suddenly stop the verses from pouring out of my heart, just as I could never stop loving him the rest of my life?

October 14, 1998

> Should I, alone, still mark the date,
> A time that once belonged to two,
> The day once used to celebrate
> The married life of me and you.
> Or is it better to forget,
> To overlook that special day
> And not go counting up the years,
> Instead subtract the pain away.
> The heart just answered. . .now I know
> What life is left, what Time allows,
> I will always keep the very hour
> My love and I exchanged our vows.

1999

The year flew by and once again
It's time for sentimental verse,
For chocolate cupids wrapped in gold,
And words of love I must rehearse.

My Valentine is ready now,
But how to send it? Must I guess
That unreal place where you have gone,
How can I know that strange address?
The wisp of cloud, the whispering leaf,
The sudden shimmer from a star
All gently speak and subtly hint
Just how you sense me where you are.
I'll stamp this letter with a kiss,
And let it drift down memory's stream.
Tonight I know you'll find it there
And I will love you in my dream.

*This was written the year
after my husband died.*

To Bud

It was a crazy dream come true,
That daring day I married you.
So many reasons said, "O no!
It won't work out, can't ever go!"
But when we kissed all reason flew
And then I went and married you.

The troubles entered right on cue,
But not because I married you.
Our income never met the crunch,
That we'd be rich was not my hunch.
But all along I always knew
How rich I was by marrying you.

When luck arrived our fortunes grew.
I had it all by marrying you,
And what for us was counted best,
Those three sweet children in our nest.
It seemed good times were just our due.
And just because I married you?

Of course the skies weren't always blue!
Did I regret I married you?
Or could I ever say goodbye,
Instead I'd black your roving eye.
Thank God there was that magic glue,
You were my man, I married you.

The years have numbered sixty-two
Since long ago I married you,
And even though you've gone away
I have to celebrate this day.
What life is left will our love renew
Because of that day I married you.

October 14, 2000

To My Husband on Our Sixty-Third Anniversary

Please take my hand again
As you did long ago.
Could years count sixty-three?
They flew so fast you know.
Please love me as I am,
A relic of that bride,
Who lost the looks of youth,
Still bloomed, though, at your side.
Please raise your glass tonight,
Our children will be there
To celebrate with us,
But who can fill your chair?
O' Darling, must you stay
This scary space apart?
It gets too hard for me
To ease my breaking heart.

October 14, 2001

The Love Rose

2001

One winter day before you died
You planted a deep red rose outside
And said, "These blooms will be the sign
I want you for my Valentine."
I tried to send you one last year,
It was no use for you weren't here.
I even tried the year before. . .
What makes me take my pen once more?
I see the day is drawing near,
My yearly purpose makes it clear,
I'll write the words and use what art
To let you know what's in my heart.
But this is hard to do, you see,
For you have gone so far from me.
Shall I address it to a star?
Perhaps the sea is where you are.
You can't answer me I know,
Or show my message how to go
But spring still comes, and winter goes,
Then suddenly I see your rose.
It lets me know this day,
That always love can find its way,
For I am yours and you are mine.
It's our eternal Valentine.

For My Husband's Eighty-Ninth

Today my tears are near, my heart is sad,
For I remember birthdays that we had,
The happy parties that went on and on. . .
There is no party here, the birthday boy is gone.

But I shall make a cake, his special kind,
And have the candles ready to be lit.
It matters not that sorrow steals my mind,
My love is strong and makes a go of it.

January 15, 2002

Valentine to My Husband

2002

When we were very young
The valentines were frilly,
The words on candy hearts
Inedible and silly.
Then once we knew first love,
The sentiments grew bolder,
We hoped the answer would be "Yes,"
Or cried on someone's shoulder.
And then there came that year
Of grown-up loves' endeavor
To claim there at the altar
Our love would last forever.

How bleak and sad this day.
We lovers have been parted,
And you were sent so far away
It's left me broken-hearted.

On Bud's Ninetieth

2003

This morning the wintery numbers on the page
Say it is your day and you've turned 90.
But

On the calendar of my heart
You are 21 and I have just fallen in love with you
Happy Birthday!

A broken heart is sad to see,

Especially if the heart is mine.

But sometimes you must let it be,

And have it for your Valentine.

February 14, 2003

Our prospects were unreal
But our love was far from phony
That day we bravely took
To the sea of matrimony.
Sharp reefs lay all around,
There was even distant thunder,
But we just set our sails
To be filled with love's new wonder.
How long the voyage has been
And how full of joy and laughter.
Some storms did come our way,
But there were always rainbows after.
Three children joined our crew,
And now grandkids add their blessing.
So how much love is there?
We'd just be second guessing.
The tide comes in, goes out,
Maybe sun and moon are paling,
But on our ship of love
You'll still find us sailing . . .

sailing

sailing

Photo Notes ⌁ The photographs in this book are from the Bridges' family archives. I have made every effort to credit any photographer whose pictures I have used in this book. However, in some cases, I don't have the necessary information at this time.
Dorothy Bridges

J ust like some of the other wonderful surprises of our marriage, to our delight, our grandchildren just happened, and we were blessed with eleven of them. ❧ From Beau's clan came Casey, Jordan, Dylan, daughter Emily, and Ezekiel. Casey is a youth soccer coach and a documentary filmmaker. Jordan is an actor. Dylan and Emily are studying film and theater in college. Beau's wife Wendy says young Zeke wants to be a stuntman. ❧ For quite a while it looked like we were mainly going to have grandsons to spoil, then Jeff's wife Susan, in quick succession, presented us with a bevy of blue-eyed blonde beauties: Isabelle, Jessica, and Hayley. Isabelle has embarked on an exciting path into the world of real estate. Jessica and Hayley both maintain straight-A's as university students. ❧ By the time daughter Lucinda married, we were ready for more boys: Marcel, Wes, and Tucker. Marcel brings his French heritage into his career as a hotelier, while her other sons are too young to know where their future lies. ❧ What I'm most grateful for is that they have been raised by loving parents who have taught them how to love, life's most important lesson. ❧ Now I look at the miracle of my first great-grandchild. Lola, the firstborn of grandson Jordan and his wife Carrie, is just as beautiful as the others, but do I sense something special about her? Isn't she saying that our family of love will be going on forever?

Acknowledgments

Thanks to my daughter, Lucinda, who masterfully orchestrated this project.

Thanks to my sons, Beau and Jeff, who guided and inspired me to publish my personal writings.

With sincere appreciation to Jana Anderson, the talented designer and collaborator of *You Caught Me Kissing*.

With gratitude to Thorsten Kaye, poet/actor, who first published my work.

Thanks to Laura Seidel, my very capable assistant, who provided indispensable support while I organized my memoirs.

Thank you, Jim Neuman, who helped get this book underway.

Each individual's contribution played a part in making this achievement possible.

Anne Morrow Lindbergh

When you love someone, you do not love him or her in exactly the same way, from moment to moment. It is an impossibility. And yet this is exactly what most of us demand. We have so little faith in the ebb and flow of life, of love, of relationships. We leap at the flow of the tide and resist in terror its ebb. We are afraid it will never return. We insist on permanency, on continuity, when the only continuity possible is in growth, in freedom, in the sense that the dancers are free, barely touching as they pass but partners in the same pattern. The only real security in a relationship lies neither in looking back in nostalgia, nor forward in dread or anticipation, but living in the present relationship and accepting it as it is now. ✍

Gift From the Sea PANTHEON

www.ingramcontent.com/pod-product-compliance
Lightning Source LLC
La Vergne TN
LVHW011359080426
835511LV00005B/354